Healing.

love letter to my life.

by
Draya Love

Published in the United States by:
Happy Living Books Independent Publishers
www.happyliving.com/books

Artwork - Jordyn Garfein
Edited - Jonathan Richard Grant
Front & back image - Froilin Abella
Audible - Christopher Deguzman

ISBN: 978-1-7321152-2-4

For permission requests, please
contact:info@drayalove.com

Printed in the United States of America

Disclaimer

sharing my experience from the
depths of my heart.
for the hope and healing of humanity.
a gem and ticket to your freedom.
let's go on a journey.

prerequisite before beginning

please
turn off your thinking mind.

no analyzing
as you take this in.

this
is
meant
to
be *felt*
and *processed in your heart.*

thank you.
i *love* you.

TABLE OF CONTENTS

The Choice to be in Love with my Life.

Glossary not to be Glossed over
        (TO BE USED AS YOU READ,
        look for the asterisked* words to guide)

Gratitude

BREAK IT DOWN

Healing is a PROCESS.

I know this.
I have spent the last eight years healing myself from a
diagnosis of fibromyalgia and lupus.
it hasn't been easy.

this *process* illuminated the need to address the neglected
internal work.
and my road back to myself.

this journey has been (and still is) incredibly complex.

it's about learning.
                                    and our *choices*.

we have a choice to suffer through it
or face it,

and see it for what it is.

We
all
need
healing.

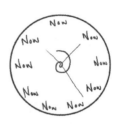

in. whatever. way.

*

This book is being written for our times.

Societally and personally,
we are hurting.
                    more than necessary.

we
don't know where to turn,
who to trust
or where to go next.

through my own experience, I have learned a lot.
it helps me teach others on their journey.
that is what this book is for.

*

Mastering

being a *non-reactive* observer in my life over
the last several years

watching things happen to me.
so I may understand the whys and the hows.

learning.
growing.
leveling up.
that's what this road is about.

understanding now how to be in command of my energy

instead of a victim to my

life
and what has
'happened' to me

      my circumstances.

see, something
has 'happened' to
all of us

      family circumstances,
      a series of rough times or lessons
      or simply,
      life.

many of our storms are worse than others.

it matters most how we handle it.
how we move forward.

options to:
learn the lesson.
be angry,
'stuff' away our experiences (inside).
        or actually do something productive <u>with</u>
                        what happened.

(for many, individual lack of action can be attributed to
non-knowing how to deal/cope/navigate through
life circumstances.)

It's about seeing the something good in the
details of
        the healing.

many times, this process can be painful.
                Horrific
                and   nonsensical.

but.
it's about perspective on so many levels.

slowing into what is
REALLY

happening.

getting control over
our reality.
whatever that may be.

*

everyones reality, so different.
And all of us understanding

                              that is okay.
that it's actually supposed to be this way…

finding and making peace.

learning to release ourselves from judgement
and expectations.

beginning with love.

on the journey *back to ourselves*.
may all of us make it home safely.

so much hope.

5

mantra. break it down.
(read out loud, hear your words)

I choose to open my mind and my heart to healing, in all ways. I am willing to see the things I have not seen. I will try to understand what my next steps are.

I release what has 'happened' to me and am willing to walk into my healing. I am ready, and excited, to journey back to myself.

HERE WE GO

What if I told you that,
"you and your life
are a physical manifestation
of what you energetically
perpetuate*."

Most
wouldn't really believe that because
                                it can be scary.

it puts *too much control* in our hands
and gives us too much accountability* for our lives.

For many of us, that could be a lot to handle.

In peeling back the layers of my life
it has been really interesting
to watch
and experience,
to process and journey through.

9

Showing me so. many. things.

Things that I didn't want to hear,
things that I *did* want to hear

and, ultimately
what I needed to hear
        to get to what was   next.

Our life.

it's this interesting
interactive* relationship with the universe.
It asks questions and gives us
the opportunity to respond.

quite a fascinating concept.
that our life is working *with* us,
a
living
breathing
interactive piece of art that we can design.

Imagine that…
an actual relationship.
        with. the. universe*.

That we are co-creating in our existence.

if that were true, (it is)
just how could it be revealing itself in your life?

having that much power?
and opportunity
to make things happen…

It sounds too good to be true, right? I know.
but I have found this in my journey:

> I can do anything I want.

finding the steps and the *hows*.

I recognized what I
had been doing to myself,
what I did to myself
    just by living in this earthly* world.

also
discovered how to *unravel* myself.

*

from the manifestation of lupus and fibromyalgia,
what it meant for me/to me/about me
about my past.

11

listening,
over several years—
discernment*, contemplation, being—
with regards to what was next.

offering a new view on healing.

(I'm going to teach you how to do this with,
and in, your life.)

I found the more
that I actually in-ter-act-ed with the universe

it would show me that it was interacting back...
in everything I did.

always bringing me to laughter.

the more I started to trust myself,
my experience(s)
and that of the co-creative* process
in which I am a part,

I was *amazed*.

I *am* amazed.

I continue to *be* amazed.

12

The universe,
this process,
my life,
each day,
the circumstances,
the ability to respond,
the choice to be happy no matter what,
the opportunity to see each see each day as a gift
and participate in the creation of my life.

is magic*.

and it's real.

Participation and co-creation
in your own experience.
talking to the universe——

a gift
we have access to
right now
and always.

simplistic to think
that doing our work,

paying attention to what's in front of us,
processing through what's in our heart,
doing what we feel most deeply,
letting our instincts guide us,
coming into our superpowers,
trusting the co-creative process of the universe...

at the end of every day,
or in the moments of every day,

can get us to (and *is*) the pot of gold

 that's, really, where the magic is.

*

So they say that there's this thing called heaven.

Many existing to 'get there.'

but. What if I told you
that

you are

already there...

Many wouldn't think it's true,
not in the collective state
and place
we're in right now.

(especially with society crumbling at every aspect
(or so it appears).)

everything falls only to be re-built
on proper structure.

and I think we're ready for some realignment…

facing this is important.

with some love and compassion

towards selves and others (Gaia too).

non-judgmental
allowing
and flowing,
learning
and growing…
coming into *our knowing*

then showing others how they do this.
(it's really a constant state of bliss).

so essential to master yourself
get to know you.

truly the most important thing we can do.

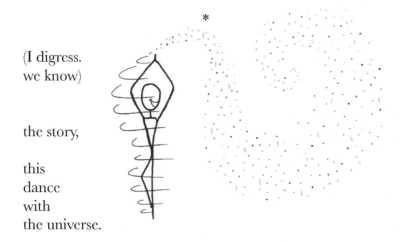

(I digress.
we know)

the story,

this
dance
with
the universe.

the joy I have found

in getting there (here).

My journey (the journey)... is so rich with synchronicities*

and knowings
and love
and laughter.

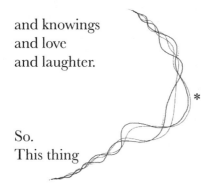

So.
This thing

called
flow*,

it's taught me so much.
trained me to get in sync
with what *is* us.

Like an interactive <u>game</u> as we live.

You see.

We think.
we plan.
we try.
we push.

THINGS TO STRESS ABOUT...

☒ Laundry
☒ groceries

☐ WORK

☒ life...

☐ fix car

☐ Make friends

but.
do we know why
        we do it?

are you aware that you can actually
                sit back

and let the universe
help?

Listen and observe, and you will hear and see.

the universe will give support. Signs exist.

17

I bet you can look back at your life/day and remember a time when…

signs were real and
when the magic *did* happen.

Open up to that. (to them)

*

Since my story got real.

when my body manifested illness.
that is when I needed to really pay attention to
how hard I was PUSHING in my life.

We aren't meant to push in the ways in which we've been
conditioned*.

(they are unhealthy and not-sustainable.)

But in listening to and addressing the chaos in my body.

finally seeing what needed attention.

I
have
learned

so
much from the lessons.

and I found
so
much
abundance and information
        in being present and living well.

(makes my heart smile so big.)

And my life

It's
a living testament

to what it is I have been through.

feeling
and peeling off.
manifesting
intentionally*,
strategically flowing

as i have surrendered.

Surrender is a big piece (of the game) that so many of us
have been missing.

it isn't supposed to be hard.
we've just been trained to think it is.

i know this and, with time, you will too.

life is beautiful
it will speak to you.

you can do what you love.

you can be what you want do what you want
have everything you want...

<u>because</u>

you already have
                everything you *need*.

you just gotta
                stay. the. course.

understand how to 'read your life.'

& you.
Really.

the journey ahead is the journey *back to you.*

and that is where I am going to take you…
all the way back to yourself

*

I have fallen in love with myself
and I want *you* to find yourself in the way in
which I found my way back to me.

This book will take you there.

revealing that it's time to
lay down the boxing gloves of life.

finally, seeing that
we.
aren't.
in.
a.
fight.

We are in a
CO-CREATIVE PROCESS
with ourselves and the Universe.
a BEAUTIFUL dance
as we learn to recognize
and participate
in ITS rhythm.

It's funny,

joyful,
hopeful,
so entertaining

such a privilege to be a part of the training.

I am
honored
to participate
and manifest
and enjoy.
I invite you to do the same.

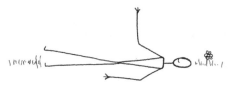

but, you gotta decide.

because it is a decision.
and a commitment.

to you.

Are you interested in examining what the
journey back to yourself would look like?

I hope so.
If you picked up this book,
you are ready to begin.

I ask you to *take your judging lenses off…*
        as you will find a lot of things along the way…

that can be distracting, even hurtful.

Remove judgement* from yourself, and others.

        simply look at things.

making the decision in your existence
not to be a reactor*,   but *the observer.*

to discern and slow down.

it's a game y'all.
I'm serious.
Life. is. a. game.
decide to play.

but——play differently.

                    *

So in the flow eight years later,
since I made the commitment to ME.

The universe is on our side.

make the choice
to get curious

about your life
and trust the process

trust yourself.

YOU have everything that you need.

Your life will speak to you
and participate *with* you
when you know how to listen, look, visualize
and see all the details in the process.

mantra. here we go.
(read out loud, hear your words)

I am ready to participate in my life and see it for the gift it is. I see that I have the power to create everything I want.

I am willing to love myself and see myself for the beautiful being I am.

I will take a chance on myself. I will trust my life and have more gratitude for this experience. Thank you.

26

PERSPECTIVE

Let's start
in our lives,
with what is in front of us.

(at least how we view it)

what is in our control.

stop and take a little inventory on what is happening
in your reality*
        right now.

what might you be able to do with where
you currently are.

                    *

How you see

and possibly view things
may need some   *adjustment*.

29

this is where, removing judgement
may be necessary.

(sit with that concept for a bit.)

What in your life
can you view differently

or

what might just be there
to speak to you
for some reason?

See, our lives
are speaking to us
individually and collectively.

Question:
What is your life SAYING to you?
    how is it attempting to communicate?

are you listening?

the answers will be different for each (all) of us.

our unique situations will help us take inventory of what
we need to be paying attention to.

what we have
and haven't dealt with.

what is in 'our space,'

just start by listening,
observing and
by learning to tune into
the unspoken details everywhere.

they will lead the way.

31

mantra. perspective.
(read out loud, hear your words)

I realize that my view is just one view. I want to remove my judgmental lenses from myself, from others, and from 'situations.' Learning to open my heart up to see things in a softer way.

Looking at things with a lighter heart is an easier, more beneficial way for me to live. Everyone is worthy of their view and their experience. I will create loving space for others to be around me, regardless of their perspective.

I will be open and loving.

33

FORGIVENESS AND COMPASSION

We are born.

conditioned
and confused.

all of us.

put out into the world to
put together the pieces of
why our life feels,

how it *feels*

to us.

learning how to navigate and comprehend it all.

examine if we've
adequately addressed the past.

many of us have messy parents with imperfect
circumstances.
(we messy too)

many of us
don't know how to shake off what
'happened' to us
or understand why.

> ('what happened' will repeat
> until we learn the lesson
> (in various forms).)

time for lenses of forgiveness.
for ourselves

and those that took us thru this matrix thus far.

they did what they could.
we are doing the best we can.

many people get stuck here.
———make a choice to move on.

with compassionate hearts,
we must forgive   *to move forward.*

start with your own heart.
listen to what's been suppressed and 'stored.'

as we are harsh on others,
it is a reflection of us being harsh on our selves.

internal chaos creates the same externally.

the world is chaotic enough.
please choose peace inside yourself.
things will go smoother that way.

(for everyone)

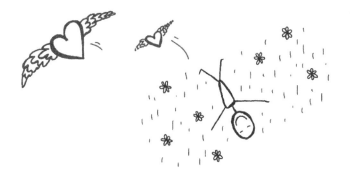

mantra. forgiveness and compassion.
(read out loud, hear your words)

My heart is full of compassion and forgiveness for myself and my fellow human. I am love, I am worthy, I am a part of the whole.

I allow myself to release old attachments and choose to move into a healthier mindset. I embody and am open to receive the compassion and forgiveness that the world needs now.

I am free.

ENERGY IS EVERYTHING

everything happening to us,
around us
is a perpetuation of energy*.

old energy
new energy
past-life energy
our parents' energy
collective energy,

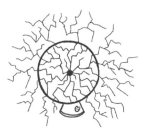

and we wear this energy in many different capacities.

many times wearing that of others
(kinda like a funky heavy old coat)
in non-visible
and confusing ways.

_____whose patterns or energy are you wearing
(_carrying)?

*

energy manifests in the world as
experiences
people
situations
circumstances
songs
thoughts
dreams
materialization* of ideas
(purposeful or not, intentional or not)

but again.

it is
all
energy.

We are comprised of it.

slowing into this understanding
can begin to
lay your *new life*.

learning

to read energy…

witnessing the physical manifestations* of what's
happening in our
'energy field'* or our selves

(we can't literally see this, just know it's there)
we have the ability to do something about this.

we MUST be open
to accountability in our life.

all egos left at the door.

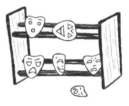

hold on and get ready to go.

this.
is.
work.

no. joke. work.

but.
you get the prize at the end.

It's.
you.

Either you are ready
and willing

to make the decision to get to that work.
or
you aren't.

and actually,

both,
all.

are okay.

people will   *wake up*
in their own time.

this is. after all.
        the Great Awakening.
entering when we allow it.

In learning to not 'push'
(I accidentally still do but
i'm working on it)

44

we are all living out
our own versions of
this reality.

we all walk
our own path.

and make the choice to
be a participant in our lives.

The world is awakening,
a new consciousness is being birthed…

        and now, it's your turn
to see what needs to be seen——
      and, ultimately, done.

only
you can do your work.

that is true for each (all) of us.

simply speaking,
we try to compensate for one another.

       as we   break away from
                 old (stagnant) paradigms.

living from our hearts,
doing our own part
and teaching our people
how to be responsible
and accountable
in their lives.
...is the best thing we can do.

and doing our best is good enough.

be a
living.
breathing.

example
of love in
your own life.

be it
walk it.
exude it

and create your own frequency
————and legacy

from it all.

nothing will speak louder in your life.

mantra. energy is everything.
(read out loud, hear your words)

I release myself from the need to understand everything. Energy is moving in my life, everywhere.

I make a choice to listen to it, participate in its opportunities, and to flow with it. I allow energy to move freely in my life so it may speak to me in miraculous ways.

I am willing to be present and curious.

CREATING YOUR OWN
FREQUENCY

become your own vibe.
(or simply being you)

Also you

Self-Reflection.
so good.
so juicy.

knowing who you are.
        what you *love*.

eventually you
will become *your own thang*.

Isn't that what everyone should strive for?

to know ourselves,

51

so greatly

that we
exude
who we are.
our own vibe
like no other

in every

waking,
breathing step
of what we do,
say,
spend time on…

working towards living the
I AM that you are.

each day. right now, in your life.

truly knowing yourself.

so
sure in you.
in how you love.
in how you feel.
in feeling. period (.)

because it's
important

significant
and key

to our happiness.

be you.
do you.
trust you.
honor you.
be kind to you.

re-parent yourself.
love yourself.
forgive everyone.
(including you.)

be compassionate and gentle. *please.*
        know how amazing you are.

know that
you are perfect
right now
and
have always been.

(we must unlearn to relearn).

know that you are exactly where you need to be
now, as you will continue to be...

Finding perfection in what you don't yet know but are
diligently listening to the whispers of...

the details, so revealing.

Silence needed. for the whispers to be heard.

مكتوب   *

there is this Arabic word,
    Mactub.

It means

it is written...

That it is
and
was already written

who you are...

why you came here...

and what

'your work'

is to be on earth.

knowing this brings much peace.

knowing what is,
just is.

becoming aware + congruent with
the you that you are,

        part of the all-inclusive I AM.

realizing it's all written in the stars.

feeling comforted,
releasing all into the universal assistance,

witnessing how much better life is when we align
with our highest, best self
is when it starts getting fun.

                    *

raising ourselves

in order to do our work in the community
and in the world.

raising (y)our frequency
and (y)our vibe
changes the world.

each
one
of
us.

getting to know ourselves, individually and collectively.

power in all of that.

changing (y)our vibe changes *everything.*

The Draya Love Frequency was born from all of this.

> (became my reality as I began strategically
> manifesting. doing my work. all about love,
> accountability, joy, community, and abundance.)

What does your frequency look or sound like?
How will your signature impact the world?

Dream, friends. It's beautiful to
believe in yourself.

I encourage you to
imagine your own road
and
promise
it will be magical.

mantra. creating your own frequency.
(read out loud, hear your words)

I know that I am special, that I am individually me.

I was created to change the world in my own way and to find my superpowers. I am grateful for my gifts and allow myself to be completely me, free of judgement.

I will try my best to love my life—to appreciate the opportunity to be deeply fulfilled by it, through it, and with it.

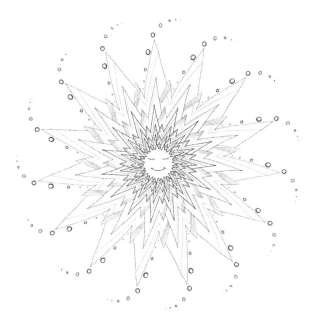

OUR RELATIONSHIP WITH
THE UNIVERSE

What does your relationship with
*The Universe/God/*Spirit*
look like?

Do you hear + communicate with a
voice or force?
Are you still?
can you tune in more?

How does it sound,
appear in your life?

Do you feel an inner knowing that
somehow always
seem to guide you in what to do?

Or maybe you've never heard it,
or it's just a strain to hear.

we can all be more present to this …

honor its presence.
allowing this to give direction in (y)our life.

It is our job to listen to
and work closely with the voice
of the universe in our daily lives.

However that shows up.

speaking individually
and guiding us to what we personally
        need to know or do   next.

it doesn't matter or have to
look like anyone else's version.
and it won't.

but.
we.
must.
communicate.
with

God*/the Universe/the God in us/Spirit/Ancestors/The
Invisible Universe…

Constantly trying to get our attention,
communicating and co-creating with us.
         (they help us get things done.)

helping
increase our belief-
faith in what we know

trust in what we hear,

intuition* to tap in
and discernment to follow.

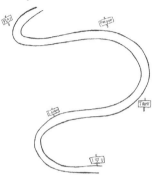

         The knowledge below the surface
         teaches us to *tap in*.

dropping deep into our knowing of what to do.
learning to listen, taking the steps to follow.

                    *

Question: Do you feel like you hear from Spirit trying to
speak to you in all sorts of ways?

Answer: (you aren't crazy, many feel that way…)

Quite often,
because it's been learned out of us
by society, the rat race,

most people don't even know how to
'hear God'
speaking in their lives…

but
God is amazing.
the Universe will show up

in any
and all ways in which
we will listen and honor it.

so, I ask,
in what ways has this energy spoken to you?

maybe it was back when you were a kid,
or maybe it was yesterday.

We are here to
'get the signs,'
listen and observe,
DISCERN the messages…

respond
and *speak*
back into the process.

showing the universe what we want out of our lives.

co-creation at its best.

(when we learn the language,
        it becomes a two-way conversation.)

the universe will speak in ALL ways, shapes and forms.
the magic of the legends and the myths has never left.

You only must listen
and be
PRESENT
to hear,
and crazy enough to believe.

*

Me?

Since I am obsessed with stones,
five years ago I was driving on the highway and the
universe heaved a stone at my windshield to give me a
message.

It left a perfect happy face in my windshield to talk to me.

        ———one of those times the voice was
    raised above a whisper.
            and, yes, I heard it loud and clear.

The rock left its mark in many ways.
        Simply reminding me to smile,
                to be happy and laugh.

we are fully supported, be sure in that.

the happy face is STILL in my windshield. thankful for
that. one of my favorite allies.

This gave me a concrete view of this universal language.
how it walks + talks, works + plays with us.

                      *

God is everywhere. the universe
omnipresent and miraculous.
witnessed in awesome and funny ways.

you just must be willing to listen.
and play along.

taking some steps into seeing the world with a
                    different view.

a world I was lucky enough to discover,
(or maybe it discovered me)?...

<u>Question</u>: what is your rock in the windshield story? how has God 'showed up' in your life?

Do you think you can get more fluent in the Universe's language? At the listening and the hearing and the observing and the speaking?

(Hint: you can.)

mantra. our relationship with the universe.
(read out loud, hear your words)

God is everywhere; including inside of me. I don't have to understand it or quantify it, just allow it and feel it.

I am open to hearing the universe speak to me. I am, and am willing to 'participate in the conversation.'

I will make time and space to hear spirit speak in my life. I will honor and listen to it.

CO-CREATION

It's quite mind-blowing to think that we have
ANYTHING
to do with what is happening right now…

but.
we do.

we MUST focus our energy.
INTENTIONALLY and STRATEGICALLY.

for we
have the ability
to create,

and if we focus the aim,
we can build more of
what we seek.

Don't get me wrong.

MOST of us have a
HUGE mess to clean up from our past.

our lives
mental
physical
spiritual…
emotional
may be a mess…

but…
with new understanding.
some kindness, gentleness and *love—*
applying patience,
we walk the journey.

it is happening.
look around the world,
      we are shifting our energy
            because <u>so</u> many people are awakening.

You are too.
slowly and steadily.

the Universe IS on our side
and wants to co-create* in
bountiful ways

that don't stress us out
and allow us to live our best lives….

*

The path of least resistance is the path of *flow*.

we must understand
and learn to live by the new narrative
that makes it
easier for us to

'live' instead of 'attain'

 'seek' instead of 'strive'

'be' instead of 'go.'

So.
co-create.
learn to listen.
be present.

interacting
with
the
universe.

it will play with you.
TEST you.

throw you curve balls...

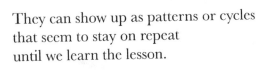

and it will help you/make you
learn your lessons...
over and over.

They can show up as patterns or cycles
that seem to stay on repeat
until we learn the lesson.

        we have the option(s) to choose
stop or continue in the cycles.

Sometimes we can learn the lessons quickly, sometimes—
intentionally or inadvertently—
                we must take the hard road...

try and make the best *intentional choices*.

we have
so much opportunity
to create
whatever it is our heart is most congruent with.

many of us
only now
learning what that is.

be patient. listen and speak.
take the time.
walk the journey.

mantra. co-creation.
(read out loud, hear your words)

I see that I am a participant in the co-creation of my life.

I am willing to look for how to do that and commit to making better decisions. I know that I have the power within myself and with the universe to create anything and everything I want.

I trust that the universe will support me in my dreams. My heart is full of hope, and I am ready to see my life with new lenses.

PARTICIPATION IN YOUR LEGACY

Changing my vibe, creating a legacy.

Where to begin.

I have found
that doing my inner work and honoring my body,
simply
this

can start the process.

it seems very basic,
        as it's supposed to be.

 but (still) it's proven true, to me.
        i believe inner work will hold key information
        for you as well.

when you begin

that inner work
and are loving
and kind to your body…
things just start
coming your way.

this requires us to participate and co-create.

daily. in all the things.

honor yourself.
your body.
your spirit.

spend the time.
choose to be present.

commit to yourself.
you deserve
to walk in
your true purpose.

and. then,
follow the path.

feel its comfort and warmth
        but don't expect perfection.

This is beautiful work.
honorable work.
The work.
　　　from which all else is borne.

the sooner we get congruent with the path,
　　　　　the less we suffer.

beginning to find our true calling.

the magic we find
when we decide.

　　　finding ourselves in all the details
　　　　　　of what we are facing.

As we are present for it all
Spirit will guide us.

We will be provided for
and supported by the universe, always,
　　　　　if and when we *participate*.

Get clear.
Be intentional.
Be specific.

　　and *be*.

Deal with your old energy issues.
(we all have them)

then *manifest* who you are: love.

purposefully create, even design
the life you want
          not the storms of everyone else.

<u>Questions</u>: What do you want *your legacy* to say about you?

          how can you begin to make it speak?

to not judge. to look outward as you travel inward?

Answer: by making the decision.
to process,
your life.

no longer repeating old histories.

mantra. participation in your legacy.
(read out loud, hear your words)

I know that paying attention to what my life and body are saying to me is the starting point.

I choose to see what the universe is trying to show me, to try to understand what it is helping me with. I will honor myself and my body, and do the work required, at this time.

I am aware of the conscious need to participate in raising my frequency so I purposefully create the legacy I intend to. I allow myself to come into congruence with my true path.

MANIFESTATIONS OF ILLNESS
(AND THINGS).

My body,
my life.

It manifested 'fibromyalgia and lupus.'
not fun.

I knew those words were just a name for something that.
energetically. had gotten
ahold of me.

the body does this, creating things.
both good and bad.
science proves this now.
                  this can be illness or situations
or circumstances in our 'energy field' that are
                  attempting to communicate with us.

It took many years—and lots of *focused attention*—to
decode* this mystery.
the doctors weren't going to tell me.

I was the only one who could figure my story out.

When I made the decision to interact with
my life.
with my body.
put her first.

finally started to honor her
and listen…

she began to speak.
(she is SO intelligent!)

she told me what all this
'illness' was.

it's QUITE a story…
for another day (another book, really)…

revealing past life trauma, family karmic ties
and   the *expression*
                        through my life. and. body.

very intense
many layers,
miraculous, unanticipated and extraordinary.

it's my story.

FEED ME!

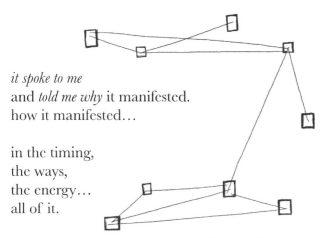

it spoke to me
and *told me why* it manifested.
how it manifested…

in the timing,
the ways,
the energy…
all of it.

when and how people, things, injuries, diagnoses
         show up   in your life—
                  what could they be telling you?

you too.
will hear the manifestations of your physicality,
the *whys* + *hows*.
                  —the little and the big things.
         (time required. <u>time well spent</u>)

I recommend
having some
deep conversations with yourself.

connecting
your higher self*,
your body.

and letting them know that you are ready.
ready to listen.
and to actually do what needs to be done

instead of ignoring the messages,
and continuing to fight

what

you know
your body
truly needs.

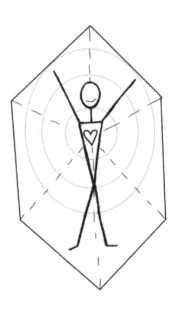

because.
only *you* know
what your
body is *begging* for.

your body.
your life,
your existence.
all
so intelligent.

so much wiser than our earthly selves.

our 3D* selves are limited,

jaded.

We *think* we know

but
simply put,
we don't.

We force
our will
on our bodies
all. the. time.

when we should

listen
to
its
will.

the body,
fighting back,
only wanting us to do what's natural.
(food, way of life, amount of stress,
lack of rest, intake of junk
(mental + physical) etc.)
          can you blame it?

We have been conditioned not to know how to

read the body's signals,
not comprehending the language it speaks to us.

some of us, who may hear it,
        even <u>refusing</u> to listen.

because that means we have to do the work
to release
what we have been holding
                and hear the trauma speak.

Ego doesn't like this. quieting down and listening to spirit.

but
it's often good
to do
what ego doesn't like.

        letting go of self-censorship to release;
                no choice really, if you want peace.

Stop the suppression.

allow your body

and life to show you
what it needs.

what is right for you.

——because, only you can
allow yourself to be lead
into its *awakened state*.

It's intriguing to know,
that we *all* get to go through this process.
(let's not forget it's a privilege)

each of us having a story waiting to be released and told.
thru our bodies…

communicating with this
beautiful vessel* we have

this 'skin suit'

that holds vibrational expression of our soul.

learn
and level-up in this game.

and discover how to
master what is *already within us*.

Make the decision to listen to your body.
it is your best ally and won't lead you astray.

It is your conduit of communication,
the path that
only you can discern for yourself.

what you think and do affects your 'skin suit.'

　　　your manifestations, manifest.
　　　only you can undo them, redirect the energy.

<u>Question</u>: what has been waiting around for you to
address?

　　　Answer: get busy listening.

The listening, the hearing, the discernment,
reveals the　　　　　　　*next in the now.*

leading you
home,
back to yourself

when you honor the process
and do what you *need to do*.

<u>And *you know*, deep down, what that is.</u>

mantra. manifestations of illness (and things).
(read out loud, hear your words)

I appreciate my body for the beautiful vessel that it is, and I make a conscious choice to listen. My body is on my side and I trust what it says to me. I will allow it to do its work and heal.

My body is intelligent, and I will do what it wants instead of what I want. I will be loving, gentle, truthful, and allowing to it.

I choose to listen to the energy flowing through, and speaking from, my body.

LIVING IN THE FLOW AND SURRENDERING

For me, the 'american way' was a part of
my conditioning.

it was to

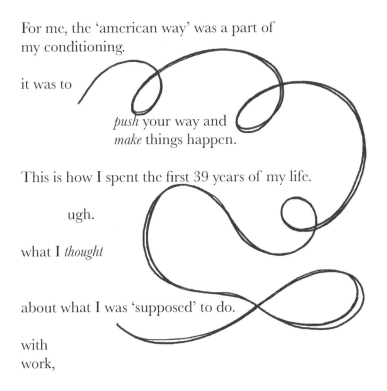

push your way and
make things happen.

This is how I spent the first 39 years of my life.

ugh.

what I *thought*

about what I was 'supposed' to do.

with
work,

family,
my body,
money,
my heart…

all of it…

thinking I
      knew better.

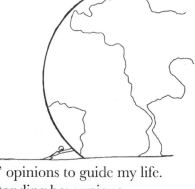

or——allowing others' opinions to guide my life.
      (not yet understanding how unique
      our journey is meant to be)

Sound familiar at all?

I believe much of this 'push'
is about early life conditioning.

about
making things happen
vs. *knowing* when things should happen

pushing vs. *allowing*

forcing our way to hear messages
                  vs. simply *tapping in.*

escaping conditioning. all. of. us.

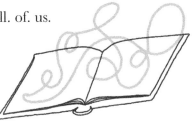

learning to be
present to
READ the FLOW.

    (it's always telling us where to go)

this effortless invisible energy, teaching and speaking to us.

helping discern what we'll know to trust.

learning to hear our truth

this flow.
        what
        is
        every day.

the 'whatever happens <u>happens</u>' when I decide to *play*.

what presents itself in our path…
(planned + unplanned)

this.

will gift the wisdom

should we choose to listen.

and learn what it is saying.

*

The flow is genius unfolding

It's actually quite complex and
if you don't yet 'get' energy
                    you might be somewhat   perplexed.

realizing there is an interaction between
          us and the universe.

this truth/knowledge
shows itself
<u>only</u> with time, practice, and presence.

watch.
respond.

strategically.

Allowing the flow to guide our path.
giving things time to unfold.

leaving room for the universe to respond to and
work with us,

showing the best avenues upon which to travel.

for flow is all knowing, it is our daily teacher.

working with it, looking at and through it
for the highest good in all situations…

that being the goal, to feel good.

always choosing to see, and reach for,
the silver lining in all.

This is what flow reveals.

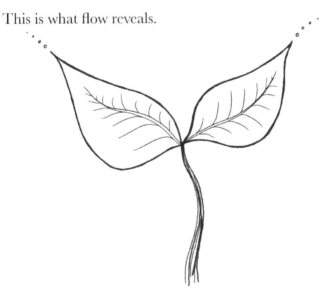

mantra. living in the flow and surrendering.
(read out loud, hear your words)

Life isn't supposed to be hard. The flow speaks to me and tells me what I need to do.

I trust my experience; I choose to listen and surrender. I release the need to know, the desire to 'force.' I will let the flow guide me, seeing the messages and filling in the details, every day.

Thank you, Universe.

FINDING MYSELF

Do you know who YOU are?

at your core,
the true, you?

Several years ago, I didn't know that answer.

      and *I didn't even know*

                 that I didn't know…

when I was
raising my family,
getting the houses, dogs
degrees, jobs
      and all 'the things.'

dealing with 'reality'
all the *distractions*.

it was really hard to see
who I was.

what I wanted.

how to hear that voice
and know what to do with that information.

I hadn't yet learned the language
                    or wanted
            to hear the conversations from
                                the Universe.

(thankfully I started to wake up)

The opportunity and decision to find myself
has been revealing in so many ways.

everything I learn has opened new doors.
and will for all of us.

                        *

My wake up came after an illness
forced me to see things differently...
(trauma helps awakening. but not necessary)

and a divorce, a door that closed to open new ones,
                    helped me clean up my energy.

plus, my kids were grown and no longer needed me
as I was accustomed to.

stepping outside these 'roles'

I was able to hear
the voice,
that I hadn't heard for so long.

it was
my own.

Question: what does your inner voice
sound like?

Answer: (   )

this inner voice.
it will give opportunity to
process your life +
do your work

and
see your shadows*.
(the hidden/tucked away parts of the self)

through listening
and deep acceptance.

109

it will speak your truth.

loving all of yourself.

in all your messiness.
all that is *uniquely and beautifully*, you.

Journey with me.
with you.
with the universe.

learning to
listen
and process.

allowing good things to come.

live in the space where we are
releasing confusion.
loving it all into the light.

finding out who we are.
what we want.
how we travel.
without all the outside influence of
other (other's) energy.

this takes time.
and can't really be rushed.

patience will be your vehicle.

as you find
you in the process
   back to you.

everything falls into place.   right. on. time.

the divine timing.

You will come to know
and see
      you can trust the universe

to find your way back. to you.

mantra. finding myself.
(read out loud, hear your words)

I see that there are many things I may not yet understand, and I am willing to allow my life to flow, willing to let it show me what I haven't been seeing.

I am willing to surrender. I am willing to be curious. I am willing to let go. I am willing to live in the moment, which is, of course, the space for miracles.

I am willing to know me because I want to know me. I am willing, and excited, to see the details emerge, allowing them to unfold.

ON BECOMING AN OBSERVER

Learning how to *not* react in your life.

We are here to
experience
and learn
from the details
in it all.

to absorb, observe, not react,
        deciding to find peace
        no matter what,

                            because *we can.*

we are meant to.

When things seem to be failing us everywhere
how do we just observe
in today's day and age,
in our time and place?

it can seem
impossible.

but it isn't.

to become the observer*, we first detach ourselves
from our physical experience on earth.

realizing how much more there is to existence,
        beyond the physical/touchable world.

Know this:

the actual story line.
right now.
we have lived before.
we will live again.

there is
so
much
more
than
now

at play.

mastery.
the learning of it,
comes through observation.
and non-reaction.

Question: do you react
or observe

or both?

———and how does that choice appear in
        your life?

When something doesn't go the way it's 'supposed to,'
how do you respond?
        could it all, possibly,
be happening for some bigger reason?

in all the things…
        how are you seeing
                and responding
                        ———and allowing?

create space for observation.
                        possibly a new view.

mantra. on becoming an observer.
(read out loud, hear your words)

I am aware. I am aware that I don't need to react as I have been conditioned to. I am aware that I don't need to react as I am accustomed to.

I can sit back, detach myself from the physical world, and see things differently.

I am aware of the need to allow room in my life for new points of view, for new perspectives.

Observation offers clarity, and the opportunity for growth.

118

119

ON MY HIGHER SELF
TALKING TO ME

As my journey teaches me,
schools me
on how things are.

my higher self
makes herself KNOWN
to me in new and evolving ways.

(she's hilarious.)

I had heard her speak before
but hadn't acknowledged the voice.

I didn't know who she was or what she wanted
for the longest time.

*

Recently I started
hearing, 'thinking'

in verse and song.

(wildly entertaining)

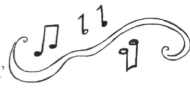

as I have been 'waking up,'
I have been watching
and observing this energy
in my space.

getting louder every year.

she's strong
and smart and silly and interactive
and magical.

I asked the universe
"what is this all about?"

the response:

my higher self
my soul
(the kinder,
gentler,
all knowing
version of me)

"she wants to talk."

and she attempts to get in touch,
in many ways…

I just hadn't listened (or been listening well enough)
before.

It is our job to link up with that voice
          (doesn't have to be an actual voice,
          (but it may for you).)
                    and work together.
in tune,
in unison.

our physical realities, and our higher selves.
Learning to work together.

We all have internal guidance
(it's free)
it's always available
          and always right.

It can and should be trusted.

Your higher
self may
sing to
you,

like mine.

maybe it speaks in riddles
or does something that
makes you laugh.

however you connect,
communication is where it's at.

two
way
communication.

it will help you immensely in your travels here.

to get congruent
with your higher purpose,
what your higher self
is saying.

We all have options to participate, to communicate,
and to believe in the messages surrounding us.

get interactive with your life and it will with you…

be playful, listen, trust, co-create.

life is so much more fun in this lane.

And, it's easier than you imagined.

mantra. on my higher self talking to me.
(read out loud, hear your words)

I am willing and open to hear my higher self show up in my life. I will align my frequency with that of my higher purpose.

I open my heart to discern what is right, for me, and am open to any way I may hear that voice. I trust my life and I trust my experience.

THE CHOICE TO BE IN LOVE
WITH MY LIFE

Life is messy.
all of ours.

many variations of how that shows up.

but being in love with our life is a choice.
        each day.

things are far from perfect.
still. I choose to be *happy with where I am*.

        We all have options and choices for
        how we play this game.

we can be all
over the place
and lost,
but. when we choose intention and strategy.

good thangs come,

all about that life.

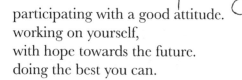

participating with a good attitude.
working on yourself,
with hope towards the future.
doing the best you can.

choosing to fall in love with our life.
makes   all the difference.

things get better.
each. and. every. day.

and that's really all I could ask of myself.
to do the work daily and be as happy as I could.

it's paying off for me deeply. profoundly. exponentially.

and on some level,
        you have already made the decision
        to be *involved,*
        and intentional in your life.

My hope is that you continue.

get curious

love
and
have so much fun, my friends.

Go do what you can

with what you have.

trust yourself. your authentic self.

be magical
all over your life.

so
much
love.

Draya Love

mantra. the choice to be in love with my life.
(read out loud, hear your words)

I have options in life.

I want the best for myself and want be happy, regularly. I know being congruent with my situation, my life, is a choice. I will celebrate the gifts every day, even if they seem small.

I will be present and see the things that are showing up for me. I choose to be involved and in love with my life. I know it will take work, but I am ready and willing.

I will observe the details—listening, hearing, co-creating—and will appreciate everything that flows my way.

GLOSSARY NOT TO BE
GLOSSED OVER

Accountability

When we decide that the things that show up in our reality are directly related to something we possibly did.

Taking responsibility for and action towards correction. No longer pointing the finger or continuing to inflict pain, trauma or drama on your own self (or anyone else).

Can be a long road. Dropping bullshit is required. Must be willing to check yourself when you are a jerk. Much energy work required for this one.

Co-create

Working with someone or something to create something greater. Learning from, linking with—and combining energies, intentions and love with other good humans to get thangs done.

Realizing I can't do things by myself and asking for help. Allowing this help and learning how to RECEIVE all the gifts. All lessons and relationships from co-creating vs. doing it all alone.

The universe co-creates with us in infinite ways. Mother earth allows us to use her energy to co-create. So much satisfaction via this method.

Conditioning

From birth we are molded by our parents, neighbors, television and 'society.' Inevitable and unavoidable, patterns are unintentionally given to us.

Our job is to observe what 'preconditioned qualities' are playing out (still) in our lives, learning which we want to keep and which we wish to get rid of.

Decode

Learning to read when language isn't tangible or visible to the eye. An ancient language that isn't visible until it is.

An unsaid language that involves learning to use our intuition and imagination to see why things are happening.

Once the basics are understood, overthinking not necessary. Spirit speaks simplistically, often very literal.

Take in everything and decipher the details that encompass the whole. Start to look at what things could mean, seeing them now as signs. Live your life and play the game with this concept.

Takes some practice, but you learn to get skilled at 'reading your life.' Then, as you get strategic with it, it gets super fun.

Discernment

Deep insight, wisdom, and knowingness. The ability to direct us towards our next step in the flow. Understanding which signs go where, when—and proceeding intentionally from there. Can sharpen this skill with practice.

Earthly World/3D

This place we live right now, this 'earth plane.' Well, we aren't from here. We are only temporary inhabitants of this incredible planet.

Let us honor this amazing experience. Earth is of the only planes that allow us to embody emotion and journey in the unique way we do; with the 'skin suits' and the lessons.

We are much more than what is happening right now, in this space, at this time. Think bigger. Think magically. Like in the storybooks, the myths. Humanity used to know and understand this, but we have had it learned out of us. Unlearn to relearn. Snap out of it.

You are an eternal spiritual-being living an earthly experience. Link in with your soul-self. Much awaits here.

Energetic Perpetuation

Something that shows up in your life, something materialized from information given/and or received, a visible or non-visible phenomenon that continues to happen via myriad of avenues in the physical and ethereal world(s).

Energy

That which runs through you. A force that will speak in various feelings and indications in your body and psyche and life.

The things you know without having to see them. belief.
Energy = truth
A force you can typically feel instead of see.

Can take some time to get in touch with, to identify this in your body and life. Speaks truth to us in all ways.

To master life, understanding energy is key.

Flow

The thing there to drop hints for us. What 'happens' in our day to show us what we need to see.

It is good for us to 'go with this.' There is magic to be found here.

Flow is all knowing and all showing, and will reveal what to do next—when we learn how to listen to it.

Higher self

We each have a higher self. Our higher soul. It has been with us, through everything. All lifetimes, all experiences, all worlds. It remembers EVERYTHING and when tapped into, acts as our guide.

We are here to link up with our higher self to be led into congruence with our physical selves.

Due to all the 'stuff' we've been through, our physical selves are damaged—but the higher self is the perfection of our consciousness. We can call on them to assist us in our journey for the highest good. A much clearer, and kinder, version of who we are.

Intuition

The invisible force that internally guides us to know what is right.

Intuition can show up as feelings in the body or thoughts via things we don't even quite know but somehow sense. Indications of what needs to be done next. (It's been called 6th sense, third eye, many other names.) Develop. Listen to. Trust.

A free internal GPS with the universe that will always lead you to the best answer. As each of our bodies guide us uniquely, everyone's intuition will sound and act differently. This innate knowingness is linked up with higher consciousness.

Intention

Thinking about what we want—and putting life, love, energy and time into making that happen.

You can 'get intentional' in whatever way works for you. Simply focus your heart and mind on a specific outcome, and give the energetic and physical time to bring it into fruition.

Must implore emotion if you want results.

Interactive universe

The universe is in constant communication, conversation even. It listens and responds to what type of energy we are 'putting out there' or manifesting.

It's always communicating with us—should we listen and believe—telling us what we need through people, places, things, circumstances, synchronicities.

Play, interact, imagine—and the universe will play along with you. (so fun.) Gratitude a MUST if you want more.

Judgement

Pointing the finger. At anyone. About anything. Your business belongs in in your life.

Tends to stem from an internal reflection of our own reality projected on other people and externalities. So watch yourself. Pray for those who are lost, and do your work.

Judgement isn't a good look for any of us. We are here to unite. Stop letting 'them' separate us; we are all one family.

Manifestation

Something that actualizes in your reality via the energy you gave it. These thoughts, beliefs and actions—purposeful or not—have the power to bring about everything from getting caught in traffic, to manifesting serious illness, to finding your soulmate. Keep your mind open.

Materialization

Something that showed up in your actual reality via situation/circumstance to tell you something. The 'why' behind the 'what' of the manifestation. Can be purposeful or not. Very energy based. Read between the lines.

Observer

The ability to watch things happen in your life without taking quick, reactive measures.

Studying, feeling, understanding all the details before you strive for an ultimate meaning. Letting things sink in so they may unfold.

The power to give the universe a little space, and time, to work on your behalf.

Personal Energy Field

The invisible energy field that we bring with us, everywhere and at all times.

The 'aura' that makes people around us feel some type of way (good or bad). It can be magical or mundane, elevating or grounding, many things.

The effect we have on others is reflective of the work we have (or haven't) done. It reveals our reality.

Many people have chaotic streams in their field, and you can feel it. They haven't 'done their work.' Others, who have worked toward mastering their energy, have a certain medicinal effect on people.

Some personal energy fields can be overwhelming, and some work in more subtle ways.

Can be a very powerful thing, either way. Do your energy work so your 'spillover' doesn't get on other people. We feel it and thank you. Clean up your energy people. It's possible.

Reactor

Pushing the gas too fast on decisions without thinking things through.

Making quick decisions and prompt action to something without giving time for thought, processing, or other possibilities. This can result in regret.

Slowing down and applying patience and discernment helps the observer quiet the reactor for better decision-making and improved forward-trajectory.

Shadow Self

A reflection of our inner lives that we may be unaware of. The things that surface to show us parts of our hidden self that may need attention.

The side of ourselves that may not be so cute that show up as parts of our personality—triggers we may become aware of in order to work through specific issues.

Working through our shadows—those deeper, more repressed things that no longer want to be hidden or

144

denied—is revealing as all can be and will guide us into our healing. Completely.

Spirit/the Universe/God

So, God aka Spirit aka the Universe speaks through one another and is present everywhere. This can be seen, felt, heard in all the ways when we are open and allow ourselves to feel what our heart is saying…

The universe is funny, amusing, weird, and so revealing—getting to know it removes our need to put 'containers' around God.

We all have God in us and around us, and have access to this energy all the time. Listen to your heart, be with community and you will see God in the interactions; Spirit is simple and will speak this way.

Allow yourself to feel God, to interact with spirit and hear the universe. No need to overthink. No need to fear.

Synchronicity

Things that show themselves in ways that make it seem the Universe is listening in on our thoughts. The universe's way of saying 'you are on the right track, keep going.'

145

When things in the physical world line up with something you were thinking or feeling (showing up right on time) like a little game with breadcrumbs and clues.

It is helpful when you learn how to read the language. Can be a cat and mouse game when you interact. Synchronize with the synchronicities in your life.

Vessel

The body that you inhabit. right now. Your skin suit.

See, you aren't your body. You *live* in your body. You are a spirit that materialized and manifested into this physical form. This vessel talks to you, teaches you, interacts with you and can be your best friend (or worst nightmare). It will tell you what it does and does not want, guiding you in every way.

Illness and negativity manifests, in many ways, in your body when you aren't listening. Learn to love, honor, listen to your body. Take the advice of this highly intelligent vessel you've been gifted during this lifetime. It's a truth teller.

Your magic

I am magic. You are magic. We are all magic. We must simply drop all our issues, deal with 'the crap' we've been avoiding to get to the good stuff.

Dependent upon: the decision to be present to, and in, your life. One must be available to see how beautiful they are as a gift to the world.

There is only one of us, each unique in our offerings. We all have special things that are to be cultivated, given light and love to. We must begin to discover that within ourselves.

The more people who open up to their magic, the more magical the world becomes. Discover your magic.

Your reality

Many of the truths we cling to depend greatly on our own point of view. How we see things dictates our reality.

All of us have completely different starting points on how and what we see. One person is not 'right' and the other is not 'wrong.'

When we slow into this understanding—respecting people's unique journeys, perspectives, and situations—we come to see that multiple viewpoints are possible.

Reality is what we make it.

the language for the new earth

Heaven on Earth

welcome to the
Draya Love Frequency.

visit drayalove.com for information,
tools and assistance on
the wake up process.
all things healing.

NOTES

GRATITUDE

This series is special to me because I had to walk in my experience to obtain these gifts. So many amazing people along the way. I want to thank a few who walked with me through this long season.

My sons, L'Rae and Jax, my gifts from the beginning. They have been my mirrors, my biggest teachers, my closest friends and the center of my heart. They have taught me more than I could ever imagine. Thank you for the truth + for the loyalty, always.

My youngest sisters, Regina and Katelynn. We have been especially close during our breakdown and rebuilding process. All of us choosing to do the challenging work amidst the pain & confusion. Our love, connection, and the commitment to healing has kept me going.

To the community—I love my tribe and couldn't have done any of this without the collective efforts of everyone supporting the project(s). The last-minute review crew was amazing! I am forever grateful for all our co-creation of love.

My editor, Jon. You are my brother from another life and have been truly divine during this process. My magical

155

artist, Jordyn. Thank you for helping my words come to life, making them more relatable and applicable. And Happy Living, my publisher. The timing and alignment was/is perfect.

And, most importantly, to *myself*—my young self, my higher self, and my current self. Making the choice to walk in your truth. It's been lonely, intense and magical in many ways. You are beautiful and worthy. Own this.

To all those who are lost in their journey of healing. I hope you find inner peace, clarity and...ultimately, yourself.

I appreciate all the people along the way. Even the ones I lost. for a myriad of reasons. All of us one another's teachers/students/teachers.

I have so much gratitude for all the lessons and experiences.

Deeply in love with my life.